SEX
AT FIRST
SIGHT

understanding
the modern
hookup culture

SEX
AT FIRST
SIGHT

understanding
the modern
hookup culture

RICHARD E. SIMMONS III

Also by the Author

Safe Passage
Thinking Clearly About Life and Death

The True Measure of a Man
*How Perceptions of Success, Achievement &
Recognition Fail Men in Difficult Times*

Reliable Truth
The Validity of the Bible in an Age of Skepticism

A Life of Excellence
Wisdom for Effective Living

SEX
AT FIRST
SIGHT
understanding
the modern
hookup culture

RICHARD E. SIMMONS III

Sex at First Sight: Understanding the Modern Hookup Culture

© 2015 by Richard E. Simmons III

Published by Clovercroft Publishing, Franklin, Tennessee and Union Hill Publishing, Birmingham, Alabama

Published in association with Larry Carpenter of Christian Book Services, LLC
www.christianbookservices.com

Scripture quotations taken from the New American Standard Bible˚,Copyright © 1960, 1962, 1963, 1968, 1971, 1972, 1973,1975, 1977, 1995 by The Lockman Foundation
Used by permission. (www.Lockman.org)

Scripture quotations taken from THE HOLY BIBLE, NEW INTERNATIONAL VERSION®, NIV® Copyright © 1973, 1978, 1984, 2011 by Biblica, Inc.® Used by permission. All rights reserved worldwide.

Cover Design by Lauren Gray

Cover Image used by permission from Andrew Georgiades, Zone Models— London, UK, and Emily McEvoy

Interior Layout Design by Adept Concept Solutions

Edited by Becky Taylor, Adept Content Solutions, and Maggie Diehl

Printed in the United States of America

978-1-939358-12-7

Dedication

*To young men and women everywhere
on their journey to find true meaning
and fulfillment in life.*

Contents

Acknowledgments

I am grateful first and foremost to my wife Holly for her encouragement and her significant contribution to the editing of this book in its early stages. I also would like to thank Jimbo Head, Kim Knott, Becky Gray and Lauren Gray for their critique and encouragement, particularly with the cover of the book. Finally, I would also like to thank Maggie Diehl for her editorial skills and a sharp eye in copyediting and proofreading the final pages.

I would be remiss if I did not acknowledge these individuals whose work greatly influenced and shaped the substance of this book. Primarily to Donna Freitas and her book; *The End of Sex*, which profoundly shaped my thinking and my perspective on the modern hookup culture. And I am grateful to Dannah Gresh and her enlightening and encouraging book, *What Are You Waiting For?* Finally, I would like to thank all the other authors listed in the resource section, whose work played such a vital role in producing this book.

Introduction

My first thoughts of writing this book began several years ago after hearing a speech by an Ivy League rugby coach. He was talking about relationships and at a certain point said, "When I listen to my players talk about their sex lives, you would think they are participating in a double X-rated movie." Then he said, "I am afraid we are going to lose this next generation of kids." I am not exactly sure what he meant when he said "lose" them, but I shuddered when I heard those words because I have three children in this very generation.

Last summer, my teenage daughter told me about a discussion she participated in at camp. She was in a cabin with ten other high school girls her age and a counselor, who was an up-and-coming senior in college, a beautiful young lady who attended a large state university. During the camp, the girls and their counselor had some very meaningful discussions. Not surprisingly, they talked about sex.

With real transparency, the counselor shared how she had been involved in what is called a "friend with benefits" relationship. There had been a guy in her life whom she would regularly have sex with, with no strings attached. It was just an activity they did together—just another form of recreation for modern day college students. She explained to these teenage girls that such behavior is very common among coeds today, but she also made it clear how deeply she regretted her decision and strongly urged them not to go down this path—it was a dead end that only led to heartache and guilt. I was stunned by this conversation.

Even then I had no real intention to write a book about human sexuality until I read a well-researched book by Dr. Donna Freitas titled *The End of Sex*. It was the subtitle, however, that really caught my attention: *How the Hookup Culture Is Leaving a Generation Unhappy, Sexually Unfulfilled, and Confused about Intimacy.* Freitas's work is an objective look at what's taking place on college campuses today. She interviewed more than 2,500 college students from all over the country through private forums to discuss their spiritual and religious leanings, if they had any, and, in particular, what, as college students, they thought about sex. She conducted an online survey, performed in-depth, in-person interviews, and collected a number of journals that students had written for the purposes of the study. Freitas believes that she had assembled a comprehensive picture of how students experience college life today. The results of her study were published in her first book, *Sex and the Soul: Juggling Sexuality, Spirituality, Romance, and Religion on America's College Campuses.*

In her second book, *The End of Sex,* she focuses with greater depth on the data as it relates to the college students' sexual behavior and the hookup culture. I must say that I came away from reading the book with a heavy heart, with a great concern for the future of our younger generations, and with a real conviction to write this book.

In the first chapter, I will briefly share some of Freitas's findings. In the remainder of the book, I will give parents of teenagers some foresight into what their children will face when they go off to college. Finally, my hope is that this book will serve as a guide to students and young adults to help them think clearly about their own sexuality.

"Today's first base is kissing … Second base is oral sex. Third base is going all the way. Home plate is learning each other's names!"

Tom Wolfe, Author

Chapter 1

THE HOOKUP CULTURE

A hookup is simply when two people accept and participate in casual sexual encounters that focus only on physical pleasure, without any type of relational commitment or emotional bonding. In most colleges today, sex has become another form of recreation that you fit into your schedule, like studying or exercising.

A hookup is not merely one possible forum for sexual intimacy among college students but has now become the expected norm. Dr. Donna Freitas observes that students have learned to merely treat each other as objects, existing for the sole purpose of providing each other a certain amount of pleasure. Furthermore, she says, "Whether the young adults coming onto our campuses want to hook up or not, they will be faced with the hookup culture the moment they walk through the campus gates."

One student explained that during a hookup, you can't allow your emotions to enter into the experience because that violates what is required in a hookup, and

---

A hookup is simply when two people accept and participate in casual sexual encounters that focus only on physical pleasure, without any type of relational commitment or emotional bonding.

---

ultimately you will pay a painful emotional price. In essence, everyone is supposed to walk away from the sexual experience as if it never happened. This is what is expected. This is what the hookup culture requires.

What strikes and disturbs me most is that a hookup is to be purely physical, devoid of emotion, and therefore should have no sense of purpose, meaning, or beauty between the two parties involved. Afterward, you are supposed to erase, or try to erase, any hint of emotional intimacy; otherwise, you will open yourself up to heartache.

The Norm

Freitas also learned from the scores of students she interviewed that the hookup culture requires students to become hardened about sex, and such hardening begins by forgetting about romance. This culture dictates that if you are a virgin, you are expected to lose your virginity as soon as possible. This is supposed to give you the freedom to enter a whole new world and forget about love, meaning, and commitment. You are now liberated to have sex with whomever you want with no strings attached.

As students become more hardened about sex, they become almost nonchalant about certain very intimate sexual acts. In *The End of Sex,* a senior female student said that kissing and oral sex are practically the exact same thing for most college students. All the students she interviewed seemed to agree that oral sex is a common occurrence during a hookup and that most girls admit they feel that they have to do it if they are really going to please a guy.

Furthermore, based on Freitas's research, it is apparent that young men are deeply involved with pornography. It is epidemic on college campuses and, as a result, guys now expect girls to perform all types of out-of-the-norm sexual acts. Consequently, they expect the young women they hook up with to perform like porn stars. They presumptuously are looking for women to give in and act like those they are viewing in their porn videos. Sadly, many of these young women are submitting to their demands. It should not be surprising that, in the hookup culture on college campuses, the idea of

---

In most colleges today, sex has become another form of recreation that you fit into your schedule, like studying or exercising.

---

dating is almost unheard of. Rarely do students go out to dinner and a movie and just spend time talking.

In her interview with students, Freitas noted that the most consistent comment she heard from students is that "nobody ever dates here." Even today, as she lectures around the country, students still complain about the lack of a dating culture on campus. Most young women conclude there is no chance they will ever find a meaningful dating relationship while in college. Therefore, they follow the crowd and end up hooking up with young men; otherwise, they fear that their time in college will be a very lonely experience.

Now this is not to say that all college students are hooking up with other students on a regular basis. But those students who go to college to have an active social life will eventually be forced to participate in the hookup culture or be left out.

People who have sex with a multitude of real or imagined partners become self-centered, superficial, soulless, compulsive, and mentally unbalanced.

Lauril Hall, Author

*Commenting on a report by the American Medical Association Council on Scientific Affairs.

Chapter 2

HOW DID WE GET HERE?

Regardless of what you think about the hookup culture in college life today, a valid question to be considered is "How did we get here?" There are several primary factors that have led college students down this path, and I believe each of these is a powerful force that impacts a student's behavior and the perspective he or she has on human sexuality.

Porn

It is quite obvious that, over the past decade, the widespread availability and social acceptance of pornography has played a major role in the rise of hooking up.

Pornography is clearly changing the attitudes of young men about the role women should play in a sexual relationship, and it impacts men's perspective of true sexual intimacy.

Porn's promise of easy, commitment-free sexual gratification on the Internet is very hard for young men to resist. In years past, to view pornography required a great deal of time, money, and effort. Today, Internet pornography is just a click away and is available twenty-four hours a day.

It is quite obvious that, over the past decade, the widespread availability and social acceptance of pornography has played a major role in the rise of hooking up.

Twenty-five years ago, only a small minority of men in college would have been considered regular porn users. Today, a majority of men on college campuses visit Internet porn sites on a daily basis. As a result and without his realizing it, a young man's view of sexuality becomes greatly distorted, for in the world of porn, women are totally submissive to men and always treat men the way they want to be treated. Therefore, many young men learn and begin to assume that the things women do in porn is how they are supposed to perform in real life. They, therefore, expect eighteen- and nineteen-year-old coeds to perform like the porn stars they watch on their computers. Additionally, they seek to persuade these young women by informing them that this type of sex is the ultimate experience because the women porn stars clearly seem to love it. In real life, if their attempts of persuasion fail, they will try to beat down the woman's resistance by comparing her to other women or expressing dissatisfaction with her unwillingness to experiment.

Pornography is powerfully shaping the sexual lives of this younger generation and is fostering this new perspective on sex.

Alcohol

Clearly, pornography has transformed the perspective young people have toward human sexuality, but there may be an even more significant force that explains the hookup culture: the abuse of alcohol by college students. In Freitas's survey of students, particularly as it relates to college social life, almost all of the students acknowledged that the number one activity on their campuses was drinking. This is a major issue that all college institutions are now faced with.

As one student tried to explain it:

I think part of it is being in college. It's such a
stressful time; there's so much going on; there's
so many expectations required. And, drinking is
a chance to relax from all that and hang out with
friends and be able to let loose. I think for some
people it's an escape—to get away from things that
are really bothering them. But I think a lot of it is just
that people are really stressed.

Drinking alcohol has always been part of college life,
but the concern today is not that students are drinking, but rather to what degree they are drinking. They
are drinking with the clear intent of getting drunk on
a regular basis. Clearly, it is this binge type of drinking that breaks down students' inhibitions. It leads them
into certain behaviors that they would never engage in
if they were sober. As one student put it, "For those
moments when you are intoxicated, you are just not
self-conscious." This remark explains an aspect of the
hookup culture—having sex with someone you barely
know because you are drunk. Listen to the words of a
young man in an interview with Freitas:

Sometimes I don't remember what happened [in
a hookup] due to intoxication. And when I wake
up next to someone, I think it was a really dumb
decision, [I] get up and leave the room hoping that

14

they will leave before I return. I usually take a shower to rid myself mentally and physically [and] never want it to happen again.

Peer Pressure

Probably one of the greatest fears we face in life is the fear of rejection. We are particularly afraid of not being accepted by our peers. I have come to the conclusion that there is one question we are always asking ourselves,

---

Clearly, it is this binge type of drinking that breaks down students' inhibitions. It leads them into certain behaviors that they would never engage in if they were sober.

---

the central question that must be answered before we will make certain decisions or take definitive courses of action. It is a question that haunts many a person's life, particularly those in college. The question? "What do people think about me?" I know this is particularly true with young men. They daily ask themselves this question in one form or another. Deep in their hearts they wonder what their peers think of them as a man. They ask, "Do I measure up?"

Think about how the question relates to the hookup culture and what a student is confronted with when he shows up on campus as a freshman. Clearly, his decisions about his social life and his sexual life will be influenced by his peers, particularly the upperclassmen. It is a defining factor that will impact the student's decisions as to the type of physical intimacy he will engage in.

Freitas says:

> Many of the women I interviewed had strong opinions of 'guy culture' on campus and spoke of how a large part of what it means to be a 'guy' is to have lots of meaningless sex for the express purpose of being able to boast about it to your friends later . . . The more hookups a guy can claim, the better off he will be in the eyes of other guys, and the more "guy-like" he will seem. The more vulgar a guy's talk about his hookups (including the ones he makes up), the more credible he is as a guy. Even if someone does not like hooking up that much, even if he feels ambivalent about hookup sex, and even if what he really wants is a long-term relationship, hookup culture requires him to act like a boy-man who is vulgar on the outside and maybe civilizable eventually. Hookup culture frowns on men for publicly expressing their feelings, showing

vulnerability, and being openly emotional. Such traits are associated with weakness and the erosions of masculinity, with many young men living in fear of this occurring to them. So men posture, perform, and posture some more.

Sadly, there is a significant amount of social pressure to conform to the hookup standards, and students who choose not to be a part of the norm will experience rejection. As a representative of the Anscombe Society at Princeton (for the stated mission of the society, see https://anscombe.princeton.edu/about-the-anscombe-society/) observed, "Those who do not adhere to, and particularly those who publicly question the tenets or practices of the hookup culture are thus considered unaccepted, unwelcome, or abnormal."

Change in Moral Standards

Another factor that has paved the way for the hookup culture is a change in how our society determines what is sexually moral and immoral. Is there any sexual relationship that is immoral today? Are there any boundaries when it comes to human sexuality? For most of our country's history, there has been one predominant worldview: the Judeo-Christian view, which holds that there is an objective moral order that has been dispensed to us by God. It is true for all people, in all places, and at all times. As God's creatures, we are called to submit our lives to His moral standards, and, when we do, it will benefit us and lead to a high quality of life.

However, there is a new morality that has slowly but surely become the predominant view, particularly with college students who are out from under their parents' authority. This modern view contends that moral truth is subjective. It comes from within the heart. It is an inner feeling. Therefore, you have to discover your own

---

So many young men are not on a quest for truth, wisdom, knowledge, and skill development. Instead, they are on a search for fun, pleasure, and happiness.

---

truth and your own morality. Once you discover what is right for you, it becomes your own moral standard. It does not matter if people agree with it, because it is your own personal moral code.

This second view of morality is predominant on our college campuses—the underlying moral philosophy that undergirds the hookup culture. It makes few moral demands on a person's life and says there really are no rules about sex. This belief is not only a philosophical statement about morality but also a theological statement that says God does not care how I should limit my lust or how I should channel my passion and desire.

One Final Observation

One last factor to be considered helps explain why young men today are having a hard time growing up, maturing, and becoming responsible adults. So many young men are not on a quest for truth, wisdom, knowledge, and skill development. Instead, they are on a search for fun, pleasure, and happiness. Their quest for a life of pleasure and fun takes priority over sound decision making that will positively impact their lives in the future. I find that many young men act like children and do not understand the value and significance of delayed gratification. They almost always choose temporary, feel-good pleasure over that which has lasting value. Most students don't understand the complexity of the human heart and its desires, which often are quite contradictory. For instance, a young man may want to excel in the classroom and have a great future career. However, he also loves to party, hookup with coeds, and stay out to all hours of the morning, making it difficult to do the necessary studying to keep up his grades. Notice there is an obvious conflict in the desire of this young man.

Our wants, while endless, are often not in harmony with each other. Modern students seem to gravitate toward experiences that bring fun and pleasure into their lives. However, wisdom recognizes the importance of discovering which desires are liberating and which are destructive. Which of my desires are in harmony with who I really am and with what I ultimately want to do with my life?

One of the most gifted writers ever is Oscar Wilde, an English author and poet. He was educated in some of Great Britain's finest schools and excelled in the Greek language. His writing earned him great wealth, and he was the toast of London. One literary critic described him as "our most quotable writer" after Shakespeare. But Wilde loved pleasure, particularly sexual pleasure, and in the process squandered all that he had, dying penniless. Oscar Wilde undoubtedly would have thrived in today's hookup culture. Before he died, he reflected on his life and penned these words:

> I must say to myself that I ruined myself, and that nobody great or small can be ruined except by his own hand . . . Terrible as what the world did to me, what I did to myself was far more terrible still. The gods had given me almost everything. But I let myself be lured into long spells of senseless and sensual ease. I surrounded myself with the smaller natures and the meaner minds. I became the spendthrift

of my own genius, and to waste an eternal youth gave me a curious joy. Tired of being on the heights, I deliberately went to depths in search for new sensation. What the paradox was to me in the sphere of thought, perversity became to me in the sphere of passion. Desire, at the end, was a malady or a madness, or both. I grew careless of the lives of others. I took pleasure where it pleased me, and passed it on. I forgot that every little action of the common day makes or unmakes character, and that therefore what one has done in the secret chamber one has some day to cry aloud on the housetop. I ceased to be lord over myself. I was no longer the captain of my soul, and did not know it.

Wilde desired to live a long life and produce great literary work. But he loved pleasure more. In the end, as he put it himself, "I allowed pleasure to dominate me. I ended in horrible disgrace." He died a broken man at the age of forty six.

It is vital that you be honest and ask yourself, "Am I on a truth, wisdom, knowledge, and skill development quest, or am I on a pleasure, happiness, feel-good quest?" These two pursuits will almost always lead in opposite directions.

"Why is there such a surge of bright, accomplished young people, students at one of the nation's best-known universities, flooding the offices of psychologists, psychiatrists, and social workers? They are looking for relief – from their crying jags, sleepless nights, relentless worrying, and thoughts of death."

Dr. Miriam Grossman, College Student Counselor

Chapter 3

THE
CONSEQUENCE

Where is the hookup culture taking this younger generation? What will life be like for them ten years from now? Will it have any impact on their future relationships, or is this a non-issue? If hooking up on a regular basis with different partners is no different from playing tennis with a multitude of partners, does it really matter? Maybe the question we should be asking is "What is really going on in the hearts and souls of young people today?"

I was recently reading a book about the rock band U2 that many consider the greatest rock band of all time. A number of years ago, as the band was rising to fame, their lead singer Bono wrote a letter to his father. In the letter he said:

> [God] gives us our strength and a joy that does not depend on drink or drugs. This strength will, I believe, be the quality that will take us to the top of the music business. I hope our lives will be a testament to the people who follow us, and to the music business where never before have so many lost and sorrowful people gathered in one place pretending they're having a good time. It is our ambition to make more than good music.

The words that strike me so powerfully are "never before have so many lost and sorrowful people gathered in one place pretending they are having a good time." Bono could easily be describing this generation of young people that is caught up in the hookup culture, looking for happiness, a sense of belonging, and yearning to be loved and accepted.

It should not be surprising this younger generation looks to sex for their sense of worth and happiness. In his Pulitzer Prize–winning book, *The Denial of Death,* Ernest Becker says that we have become a secular culture that considers God to be irrelevant to modern life. The common belief today is we are here by accident; we do not have any real purpose in life and are, therefore, seeking something to give us a sense of significance. Becker says people today are looking to sex and romance to get a sense of meaning that we used to get from God. But the problem is that it's not working. Our young people are not finding the happiness and quality of life they are seeking by having numerous sexual liaisons.

One of the common responses Freitas got from the students she interviewed is how sad and unhappy

---

> # Becker says people today are looking to sex and romance to get a sense of meaning that we used to get from God. But the problem is that it's not working.

---

they are about hooking up. They all fear that it will rob them of healthy, fulfilling sexual relationships in the future. In Freitas's own words, "At its very worst, hooking up made students feel miserable and abused, and some students claimed that all it took was a hook-up gone wrong and your college experience could be ruined—that one night could make or break your life at college for good."

So many of the students regret the missed opportunities of relationships that could have been.

She goes on to say:

> [O]n a personal level, most of these same students didn't want to be thought of merely as someone to have sex with after a night of drunken partying, or someone to walk away from without a care. Men and women both spoke of how they wanted to be made to feel special, to experience what it was like when someone else wanted to know everything about them. They yearned for someone to make an effort to create a beautiful setting in which such knowing and being known could occur, for someone who would set aside lavish amounts of time for this to take place. That women and men harbor secret wishes for what appear to be the old-fashioned trappings of romance seems symptomatic of hookup culture's failings. What they want is everything that hookup culture leaves out. The hookup is not liberating at all if what young men and women really want is to go out on dates.

The Impact on Young Women

Counselor and best-selling author Dannah Gresh has spent a large part of her adult life picking up the pieces of girls who are in deep pain because of the wounds of their sexual encounters with young men. So many of them have needed months or even years of intense counseling because their sexual relationships left them hollow and broken. They were seeking fun, desired to be accepted, and conformed to what everyone else was doing. However, after the hookup experience, they were left only with the sober reality that they had been used. Gresh writes convincingly:

> After counseling hundreds of deeply wounded girls, I have no doubt in my mind that a chemical bond is created between you and any person you have sex with—whether you consider the relationship nothing more than a friendship or whether you have been deeply emotionally connected. There's no way around it. Having sex bonds you to each other.

It's interesting that even liberal feminist Naomi Wolf believes the new sexuality is having a devastating impact on young women. She says, "The message young women heard was 'just go for it' sexually . . . We have raised a generation of young women, and men, who don't understand sexual ethics. They don't see sex as sacred or even very important anymore. Sex has been commodified and drained of its deeper meaning."

She is correct. Sex has become a commodity. For so many college students, sex is reduced to an exchange of bodily pleasure between two people: "I am not in this relationship for you but in it for what I can get from you.

You are nothing but an object whose purpose is to give me pleasure." It is no wonder that young women feel so used and worthless.

What a Man Wants

Most people believe that guys are able to make out like bandits, getting what they want from young women and then moving on with their lives with no sorrow or regret. Yet such is not the case when young men reveal their true thoughts and feelings about the hookup culture. In her interviews, Freitas assumed that college guys

> "The hookup is not liberating at all if what young men and women really want is to go out on dates."

loved hooking up with no strings attached. However, as young man after young man came through the interview process, she was surprised that almost all of them were just as stressed out by the hookup culture as the women were. More specifically, they were ashamed of their behavior, and they, like young women, desired love, romance, and dating relationships. They acknowledged that they went along with hooking up because that is what they perceived "real men" were expected to do.

Freitas then concludes her observation of what is going on in the lives of these young men with these words:

> In all of my research and visits to campuses in the past several years, I have found that men are the most talented actors of all within hookup culture. They have been taught to appear sex-crazed and reckless, even if what they really feel is something else. The idea fostered in American culture that young men are hypersexual is largely false, and therefore a destructive stereotype to maintain. It not only perpetuates hookup culture on campus but also stunts the ability of young men to grow emotionally. It teaches them to silence their real feelings and desires, which also keeps them from finding fulfilling romantic relationships. Men lose so much from these cultural misperceptions, maybe even more than women do, because at least women are allowed to speak about these feelings without having to worry about putting their femininity at risk.
>
> Our view of men and masculinity in America is not only deeply flawed and misleading but disastrous for the psyches of young men. It interferes with their ability to mature and develop emotionally as well as to express emotion, to have healthy and fulfilling relationships and sex lives, to communicate

emotional pain when they experience it, to feel empathy, and to do all these things without believing that by doing so, they are imperiling their standing as men. Women experience glass ceilings just about every way they try to move, but men also face an emotional glass ceiling. We ask that they repress their feelings surrounding their own vulnerabilities and need for love, respect, and relationship so intensely that we've convinced them that to express such feeling is to have somehow failed as men; that to express such feeling not only makes them look bad in front of other men, but in front of women too. And we do all of this on college campuses, where we imagine that students will open up and grow into who they really are. Within hookup culture, no one really wins, but perhaps men lose most of all.

Most of the major social ills in America are caused by, or fueled by, the misuse of our sexuality. If issues related to sexual impurity— teen pregnancy, addiction to pornography, AIDS and other sexually transmitted diseases, abortion, the psychological effects associated with abortion, sexual abuse, incest, rape, and all sexual addictions—were to suddenly disappear from society, imagine the resources we would have available to apply to the handful of issues that would remain.

Andy Stanley, Author

Chapter 4

THERE IS MORE

Undoubtedly, the current sexual environment is having an emotional and psychological impact on college students. But there is more. A very experienced, well-regarded counselor told me recently that pornography is the 500-pound gorilla in the world of addiction. He says that it is easy to hide from others, is very difficult to overcome, and can have devastating effects on your relationships and your future sex life. Many young men, and even some young women, are graduating from college heavily addicted to pornography.

We are only now beginning to understand how pornography is influencing regular users, particularly those who have been viewing it for a number of years.

There are those who have argued that pornography has no effect on those who consume it, but that's like arguing that people are not influenced by what they see. The advertising industry will tell you without question that what you see enters your mind and your heart and impacts who you are and what you do.

Sex therapists and educators Wendy and Larry Maltz have authored a very well-researched book titled *The Porn Trap*. They share how people are shocked when they first hear about the destructive force of pornography. So many consider it just to be harmless fun. They do not believe something that is not a drug, or a drink, or an actual sexual experience can cause such devastation. The Maltzes put it this way: "The truth is, using pornography can make you so blind—blind to the power and control it can eventually have over your life."

Pornography has a major impact on brain chemistry. It stimulates an area of the brain that is known as the "hedonic highway," whereby a chemical called dopamine is released when someone is sexually aroused. Pornography causes a huge spike of dopamine production in the brain. Many researchers believe that the dramatic increase in dopamine caused by the viewing of pornography is similar to that of the high someone experiences when he or she takes crack cocaine.

The Maltzes make it quite clear:

Porn's power to produce experiences of excitement, relaxation, and escape from pain make it highly addictive. Over time you can come to depend on it to feel good and require it so you don't feel bad. Cravings, preoccupations, and out-of-control behavior with using it can become commonplace. Porn sex can become your greatest need. If you have been using porn regularly to "get high," withdrawal from porn can be as filled with agitation, depression, and sleeplessness, as detoxing from alcohol, cocaine, and other hard drugs. In fact, people in porn recovery take an average of eighteen months to heal from the damage to their dopamine receptors alone.

Pornography can easily give a person an easy escape from real life and all of its pain, but it creates all types of problems, many of which evolve slowly so that you never really see them coming until they are quite serious. The most alarming consequence is that it causes sexual desire and functioning difficulties, and it often shapes one's sexual interests in destructive ways.

Naomi Wolf, writing in an article titled "The Porn Myth" in *New York* magazine, says, "You would think porn would make men into raving beasts." She says, "On the contrary, the onslaught of porn is responsible for deadening male libido in relation to real women, and leading men to see fewer and fewer women as porn worthy. Women are not having to fend off porn crazed men, but are having a hard time keeping their attention."

Dr. Ursula Ofman, a Manhattan-based sex therapist, says that she's seen many young men coming in to chat about their porn-related issues.

> It's so accessible, and now, with things like streaming video and webcams, guys are getting sucked into a compulsive behavior. What's most regrettable is that it can really affect relationships with women. I've seen some young men lately who can't get aroused with women but have no problem interacting with the Internet.

Journalist Pamela Paul, in her well-researched book, *Pornified*, says:

> While some men try to keep pornography and real sex separate in their heads, it's not so easy; pornography seeps in, sometimes in unexpected ways. The incursion can even lead to sexual problems, such as impotence or delayed ejaculation.

Sex therapist and psychologist Aline Zoldbrod is convinced that many young men are going to be terrible lovers because of pornography. Too many men assume that women will respond to them as the porn stars do in the videos. She says they are in for a rude awakening and will make horrible lovers because they do not know how to relate to a real woman.

Dannah Gresh, in her book *What Are You Waiting For?*, shares a common delusion that most young people have about pornography: the belief that their issues and problems with porn will go away when they are married. Many young women hope that is true of their fiancés who are hooked on porn. Gresh says this is the number

> ## Porn's power to produce experiences of excitement, relaxation, and escape from pain make it highly addictive. Over time you can come to depend on it to feel good and require it so you don't feel bad.

one question she gets from young people. She writes, "But the lure of porn is never quenched by marital sex because porn has almost nothing to do with real love and real sex. It's as counterfeit as a counterfeit can be."

Author Nate Larkin in very simple terms says that pornography corrodes all relationships between men and women because lust kills love. He goes on to say,

"Love gives; lust takes. Love sees a person; lust sees a body. Love is about you; lust is about me and my own gratification. Love seeks . . . knows . . . respects. Lust couldn't care less."

Supermodel Christie Brinkley is considered by many to be one of the most physically beautiful women in the world today. She is a three-time *Sports Illustrated*

Too many men assume that women will respond to them as the porn stars do in the videos. She says they are in for a rude awakening and will make horrible lovers because they do not know how to relate to a real woman.

Swimsuit Edition cover model. She was married to architect Peter Cook, who had a $3,000-a-month porn habit, which may or may not have contributed to his having an affair with a teenager. Cook was married to one of the most beautiful women in the world but still looked to porn to satisfy his sexual desires, and it destroyed his marriage.

The bottom line: Porn satisfies lust, not love. Lust is about me and my own satisfaction. In the end, porn destroys relationships and love.

Sexually Transmitted Diseases (STDs)

There is another serious consequence that the hookup culture is causing—the rapid rise in sexually transmitted diseases. When college students are talking about their sex lives or bragging about their conquests, they rarely talk about this subject. It is a neglected reality that needs to be confronted and understood. Forty years ago there were two sexually transmitted infections to contend with. Today there are at least twenty-five, and the number keeps growing. You have to wonder what other STDs are incubating that will be discovered tomorrow.

In her book *Unprotected,* Miriam Grossman, a psychiatrist in the UCLA Health Service, reports in one study that 43 percent of college coeds who went in for their yearly exam were shocked to hear they have HPV (human papillomavirus), otherwise known as genital warts, which can cause certain cancers. She wonders why so many students, who have generally been through sex education and have heard all about the importance of practicing safe sex, end up with HPV. Although student health services across the country work frequently to prevent sexually transmitted diseases, the surge in STDs is due largely to the reckless hookup culture.

Grossman goes on to say that HPV is so common and so contagious in the college population that most young women are infected after having sex with only one or two partners. She points out to all young college women in particular, "You'd be wise to simply assume your sexual partners have HPV infection."

Herpes is another common STD that is also quite contagious. What most people don't know is that herpes is not curable. It is with you for life. All students should think twice about their sexual behavior because one day they may bring a sexually transmitted disease into their marriage, and pregnant women may transmit the disease to their unborn children.

The Influence of Alcohol

I am not going to spend much time addressing the issue of student alcohol consumption, which I also discussed in chapter 1. But I will say that as I look back over my life, particularly my days in college, I have concluded that a large percentage of those who drink heavily and regularly during their college years generally become alcoholics.

For this reason if you do not limit your intake of alcohol now, you will likely become addicted. Once addicted to alcohol, you will be faced with two choices. Either you give up alcohol completely, or choose to remain in your addiction. An addiction that will eventually control your life, while destroying your family re-lationships, your ability to do your work, and finally your health. These are the choices you will have.

So you, as a collage student, must understand that the decisions you make about alcohol now will determine how it handles you in the future.

A Final Word

I have a final word, primarily to the young men reading this book. Too many of you are graduating from col-lege and beginning your life out in the real world with

---

All students should think twice about their sexual behavior because one day they may bring a sexually transmitted disease into their marriage, and pregnant women may transmit the disease to their unborn children.

---

two heavy burdens weighing you down. More and more young men enter their adult lives with a double addic-tion to pornography and alcohol. If this is true in your life, you have dug yourself into a deep hole that will be very difficult to climb out of. These two addictions in tandem will make it difficult for you to take life seriously, to be responsible in a career, and to function as a healthy husband and father. I urge you to hear this loud and clear: The choices you make in college in all likelihood will determine the ultimate outcome of your life.

"The massive unleashing of sexuality which is occurring in Western civilization is a reflection of cultural decline. It is well-known that an inverse relationship exists between indiscriminate sexual expression and cultural excellence."

Dr. Harold Voth, psychiatrist

Chapter 5

THE EVIDENCE

Some of you may be skeptical of what you have read thus far. You may believe that I have exaggerated my reporting, and even if the hookup culture actually exists, it is not nearly as pervasive as I am describing. Maybe most of the college students you know seem to be good kids who, by all appearances, have their lives together. But do they?

In this chapter I want to briefly share with you some of the facts and statistics I stumbled upon as I researched this book. As you will see, there is a great deal of information available that fully supports my findings, but no one seems to be paying much attention.

In *The New Harvard Guide to Psychiatry,* edited by Dr. Armand Nicholi, there is a chapter on adolescence, written by Nicholi, a professor of psychiatry at Harvard Medical School. In this compelling chapter, he details some of the destructive psychological and health consequences of the sexual revolution of the 1960s, '70s, and '80s, as well as youth sexual promiscuity. He says:

> Many who have worked closely with adolescents over the past decade have realized that the new sexual freedom has by no means led to greater pleasures, freedom, and openness; more meaningful relationship between the sexes; or exhilarating relief from stifling inhibitions. Clinical experience has shown that the permissiveness has often led to empty relationships, feelings of self-contempt and worthlessness, an epidemic of venereal disease, and a rapid increase in unwanted pregnancies. Clinicians working with college students began commenting on these effects as early as 20 years ago. They noted that students caught up in this new sexual freedom found it "unsatisfying and meaningless." . . . A more recent study of normal college students (those not under the care of a psychiatrist) found that, although their sexual behavior by and large appeared to be a desperate attempt to overcome a profound sense of loneliness, they described their sexual relationships as less than satisfactory and as providing little of

the emotional closeness they desired . . . They described pervasive feelings of guilt and haunting concerns that they were using others and being used as "sexual objects."

❖

The National Survey of Counseling Directors conducted a study, interviewing 6,500 adolescents. All 6,500 were sexually active teenage girls. They learned that sexually active teenage girls are three times more likely to be depressed and nearly three times as likely to attempt suicide as young women who are not sexually active.

❖

Jean Vanier, a very well-known Catholic philosopher, theologian, and priest, founded the worldwide l'Arche communities. (For more on l'Arche communities, see http://www.larcheusa.org/). As a Catholic priest, he admits that his life of sexual celibacy is at times very difficult, but he says that as he listens to young people pour out their souls in confession, his own suffering is nothing compared to those who are sexually active without responsibility or commitment. It is only afterward that they realize how relationships based solely on sex are unsatisfying and often result in a profound loneliness.

❖

Dr. J. Budziszewski has been a professor of government and philosophy at the University of Texas for thirty-three years. He teaches courses primarily in ethics and political philosophy. He has spent much of his time interacting with students and has observed how young women make the grave mistake of thinking they can snag a man and keep him by giving him the sex he desires.

Dr. Budziszewski writes specifically about four pitfalls along this path:

> First, ironically, in a budding college relationship, sex tends to make the relationships worse, not better. Instead of spending quality time together, going to movies, eating dinner, having endless conversations, now sex becomes predominant in the relationships. That is what is on his mind, always. You end up having sex more and more, but enjoy it less because it is taking the place of the relationship.
>
> Second, although it may be politically incorrect to say so, a man will never set a higher value on you than you set on yourself. He might have sex with a woman who tumbles into bed easily, but he's not likely to marry a woman who tumbles into bed easily. Why should he? He'd always be wondering who you might tumble into bed with next. So do you really want to be his practice doll?
>
> Third, the more you give him sex, the more you'll expect from the relationship, because that's how

most women are made. The problem is that most men aren't. The greater your expectations, the more he'll resent them because, outside marriage, he doesn't have any commitment.

Fourth, variety is typically more intriguing to men than it is to women. I know it isn't fashionable to say either, but it's true. So the more you give a guy sex, the sooner he'll get bored and find someone else to sleep with.

College of the Overwhelmed is an intriguing book that came out several years ago. One of the authors, Dr. Richard Kadison, is the chief of Mental Health Services at Harvard and a national expert in the field of campus mental health. The opening lines of the book are quite revealing: "This is a book about the extraordinary increase in serious mental illness on college campuses today and what we can do about it." The book goes on to explain how college students are stressed out. They have left the security of their homes, face academic competition, are dealing with new relationships, and are confronted by all types of cultural expectations. For many students, it becomes more than they can handle, and for this reason you see a dramatic increase in depression, eating disorders, substance abuse, and suicide. It's no wonder that today's students are drawn to pornography, alcohol, and hooking up. For so many, they serve as a means to medicate the pain and immense pressure in their lives.

———— ❖ ————

More than 1 million abortions take place in the United States each year, 52 percent of which are performed on women under the age of twenty-five. But rarely is there talk about the lasting emotional issues women have to contend with. Even Planned Parenthood acknowledges that some women experience severe psychological problems after having an abortion, even years after the actual abortion. Ironically, women report much more anguish and regret two years after an abortion than they do one month after the event.

Psychiatrist Miriam Grossman says that a majority of the women under twenty-five who have abortions are college students. Specifically, younger women who have abortions are much more likely to have lasting emotional difficulties. She recounts how often young women burst into tears over the guilt and regret of having an abortion. Many of them cannot even utter the word *abortion*.

———— ❖ ————

In a study that was cited in a federal report on pornography, a number of men were shown pornographic films for ninety minutes a day, five days a week. With the passage of time, they began to experience less sexual arousal and interest in similar materials that they were viewing. Journalist Pamela Paul, commenting on this study writes, "What initially thrills eventually titillates, what excites eventually pleases, what pleases eventually satisfies. And satisfaction sooner or later yields to boredom."

❖

Dr. Freitas reports from a study of students and alcohol consumption, titled "Risk Factors and Consequences of Unwanted Sex among University Students: Hooking Up, Alcohol, and Stress Response." The study revealed that:

> Approximately 26 percent of college students in their first and second years of college had had sex with someone they had just met when they were under the influence of alcohol; 40.4 percent had had sex with someone they knew, but with whom they were not in a relationship, while under the influence of alcohol. The accompanying statistics on sexual assault on campus in this study were startling. Approximately 44 percent of the women participating in the study reported at least one unwanted sexual encounter while in college, and 90 percent of this unwanted sex took place during a hookup. Of all the

reported incidents of unwanted sex, 76.2 percent involved alcohol, which played a significant role in blurring the lines of consent. The researchers found that often, the victim did not really remember what had happened after waking up the next day.

❖

One of the best-selling books on sexual freedom and sexual liberation written in the last fifty years was *Open Marriage: A New Lifestyle for Couples* by anthropologists Nena and George O'Neil. In one sense, they approved of hookup sex for married couples, believing that you should be allowed to engage freely in extramarital sex with whomever you please. The O'Neils believed that the Judeo-Christian traditional marriage system was outdated. Yet five years after the book became a national bestseller, Nena O'Neil completely changed her mind. So many of the couples they spoke with who experimented with consensual adultery found the results to be disastrous. She recognized there is a price to pay for unrestrained sexual activity.

❖

Dannah Gresh shares some very interesting scientific information about the human body that supports the dangers of hooking up. She says:

The limbic system is part of the basin [of the brain]
that stores and classifies odor, music, symbols and
memory . . . the brain chemicals associated with
sex wash over the deep limbic system during a wide
variety of romantic experiences. Holding hands,
the smell of perfume, listening to music, embracing
and most powerfully, the act of sexual intercourse;
work together to create a cocktail of chemicals that
records memories deep in the emotional center
of your brain. (That is why we remember sexual
experiences and images so clearly).

She then explains the role of dopamine, a chemical
released that creates a sense of pleasure. Any time your
body experiences pleasure, the limbic system gets flood-
ed with dopamine, and it makes you want that pleasure
more. It creates addiction, whether it is something good
or something harmful.

Gresh goes on to say that the limbic system was created to store sexual memory and emotion for us, and
dopamine emotionally attaches you to the source of
pleasure. This is the way God made us. The purpose
of the limbic system and dopamine is to turn our great
desires and passions into a deep, lasting attachment—
into knowing and being known. This is God's plan for
sex—unifying two people in the permanent covenant
relationship of marriage.

You can, therefore, see when you hook up with someone or have a friend-with-benefits relationship, it distorts your mind and emotions. This explains why students struggle so much in the hookup culture. We are designed to bond with those we have sex with. But college students, who are seeking fun and acceptance, find themselves bewildered over the emptiness and unhappiness they experience after a meaningless sexual encounter.

❖

In Freitas's research, she intentionally visited a variety of colleges, from private secular and public colleges to various religiously affiliated colleges. As far as the hookup culture was concerned, all of these colleges were essentially indistinguishable, except for the more conservative evangelical colleges. She says that the hookup culture does not exist at these institutions. Instead, you see real desire for restraint among these students. There exists a heterosexual culture that revolves around waiting to have sex until they are married.

My research also indicates that this same attitude exists among students who are involved with campus Christian ministries at major universities. Though they experience sexual temptation like all other students, they seek to follow the biblical standard relating to sexuality.

❖

Back in 1934, prominent scholar J. D. Unwin published a book titled *Sex and Culture*. Unwin had spent many years closely studying eighty-six different civilizations. His findings startled many people, including Unwin himself, as all eighty-six demonstrated a direct tie between absolute heterosexual monogamy and the "expansive energy" of civilization. In other words, sexual fidelity was the single most important predictor of a society's ascendancy and strength.

Unwin had no religious convictions and applied no moral judgment. "I offer no opinion about rightness or wrongness." Nevertheless, he had to conclude, "In human records there is no instance of a society retaining its energy after a complete new generation has inherited a tradition which does not insist on pre-nuptial and post-nuptial sexual restraint." Clearly, civilizations flourish when they demonstrate premarital sexual restraint and faithfulness and fidelity in marriage. For Roman, Greek, Sumerian, Moorish, Babylonian, and Anglo-Saxon civilizations, Unwin had hundreds of years of history to draw upon. He found there were no exceptions. These societies flourished, culturally and geographically, during eras that valued sexual fidelity. Inevitably, sexual standards would loosen, and the societies would subsequently decline, only to rise again when they returned to the more rigid sexual standards.

Unwin seemed at a loss to explain the pattern. "If you ask me why this is so, I reply that I do not know. No scientist does . . . You can describe the process and observe it, but you cannot explain it."

Philip Yancey, after reading Unwin's book says:

> Unwin preached a message that few people want to hear. Without realizing it, though, Unwin may have subtly edged toward a Christian view of sexuality from which modern society has badly strayed. For the Christian, sex is not an end in itself, but rather a gift of God. Like such gifts, it must be stewarded according to God's rules, not ours.

Christianity teaches that there is a divinely established moral order and that we as human beings just can't decide for ourselves what is moral. When we choose to defy God's moral order, there is a price that we pay.

❖

I close this chapter with some powerful words of the popular author Eric Metaxas: "What matters is the idea that some things are so sacred, that they cannot bear unveiling. Because we live in a culture where mystery has lost its value, where to hide something is often thought of as merely repressive, we don't understand this idea of 'the sacred.' We seem to have accepted the fashionable idea that all things once thought sacred and mysterious—sexuality most notably—must be freed from their mystery and 'sanctity.' But in most cultures throughout history, the opposite has been true. Most cultures have a pronounced reverence for the sacred, which they veil out of deepest reverence and respect."

"*For many [students], their souls are running amuck and their life is in chaos. They are living off of incoherent dreams and illusions. Enslaved to their desires or their bodily habits or blinded by false ideas, distorted images, and misinformation, their soul cannot find its way into a life of consistent truth and harmonious pursuit of what is good. Normally, unfulfilled desires and poisonous relationships are the most prominent features of such lives.*"

Dr. Dallas Willard, College Philosophy Professor

Chapter 6

WHAT ARE THE RULES?

While Dr. Donna Freitas was delivering a lecture, a young woman in the audience raised her hand and with great sincerity asked her why she was making such a big deal about sex. She asked, "Why does sex have to be any different than, say, taking a walk by myself? What distinguishes sex from all other things we do that aren't such a big deal?"

Most of the other students disagreed with the young woman; they thought sex was a big deal. The problem, however, was no one could articulate why they felt this way. The exchange then led to a discussion with the students on the meaning of sex and what they thought was good sex. Dr. Freitas was surprised that none of them had given a whole lot of thought to this. Here are some of the questions she asked them:

"What would good sex feel like? Who would it be with? In what kind of setting? Would you want to have sex with some kind of commitment? If so, why? If not, why not?"

It was astounding that these questions were foreign to their college experience. They had a hard time imagining what good sex might entail. Until that moment, it was as if it had not occurred to them that they not only had a right to ask these questions, but also owed it to themselves to do so.

Freitas realized that all these students had never given much consideration to the meaning of sex and to the idea that the hookup culture is all about repressing romantic feelings and romantic love.

Our Ideas about Life

All of us, whether we realize it or not, are in the process of trying to make sense out of life. As we grow up and mature, we begin to develop ideas of how life works. These ideas are important because they have such a significant impact on the choices and decisions we make.

When students arrive on campus, their thinking begins to be influenced by their professors and their classmates. There is a sense of intimidation particularly among freshman when they show up for the first day of class and begin to experience college life. It is generally the first time their parents have little or no direct influence over them. Their worldview and their ideas are shaped more profoundly during these four or five years than at any other time in their lives.

However, one of the things we can learn from philosophy is that our ideas about life and how it works can be true or they can be false. Additionally, if we live with false ideas about reality, the result can be devastating.

> . . .young people are finding their lives damaged emotionally, psychologically, and physically because of the ill-advised decisions they have made with their bodies.

Albert Einstein believed that French mathematician and religious philosopher Blaise Pascal was one of the most brilliant men who ever lived. Pascal said that the primary reason people struggle in life is that they have false ideas about reality. For this reason, he believed that if you want to live a full and satisfying life, you must uproot your false ideas and replace them with truth and wisdom. False beliefs can be catastrophic. Often, we are unaware that a particular view of life is not simply wrong but also destructive. It's not until we get burned that we might begin to reconsider that belief, especially when it comes to sex and sexual intimacy.

The Laws of Life

Before considering the meaning of sex, it's imperative to examine a very important and pertinent principle. Life is governed by certain laws and principles that are not necessarily good or bad, moral or immoral; they are simply true. However, what is so crucial for us to grasp is that principles actually make life predictable. Such an understanding creates the potential for more predictable outcomes in our lives. Most significantly, our lives will flourish when they are in harmony with these principles.

Stephen Covey writes in his bestselling book *The 7 Habits of Highly Effective People:*

> Principles always have natural consequences attached to them. There are positive consequences when we live in harmony with the principles. There are negative consequences when we ignore them. But because these principles apply to everyone, whether or not they are aware, this limitation is universal. And the more we know of correct principles, the greater is our ability to live wisely.

WHAT ARE THE RULES?

By centering our lives on timeless, unchanging principles, we create a fundamental paradigm of effective living.

Covey is clear that you cannot violate these fundamental principles with impunity. Whether we believe them or not, these unchanging principles have proven to be valid throughout all of human history.

Let's consider the "The Double Power Principle," which I first read about in a book by former Notre

> ## It is difficult for modern sophisticated people to believe that the biblical teaching on human sexuality offers the fullest, most satisfying sex life.

Dame professor of philosophy Dr. Tom Morris. The principle is simply that "the greater the power anything has for good, the greater the power it correspondingly has for evil." Take, for example, nuclear power. When it is harnessed and is used to generate electric power, it can efficiently produce energy for our homes and businesses. However, when used to make an explosive device, it has the potential to kill millions of people.

The Double Power Principle has another application. "The greater the power anything has for joy in this life, the greater the power it also correspondingly has for pain." A number of wonderful things bring such joy and goodness into our lives when they are used and enjoyed the way they are intended. But when these same gifts are misused and abused, they can bring much pain and sorrow into our lives. This is particularly true of sex. I truly believe that sexuality is one of the most meaningful and powerful sources of joy and delight in this life—but only when you experience it the way it is designed.

When sex is misused and abused, it is the source of unbelievable pain and heartache. And as Freitas and Grossman have observed in their conversations with college students, young people are finding their lives damaged emotionally, psychologically, and physically because of the ill-advised decisions they have made with their bodies. This is what the hookup culture has produced.

The Meaning of Sex

George Leonard is an American author and educator who died in 2010. He wrote fifteen books and at one time was editor of *Look* magazine. For a number of years, Leonard was a big proponent of the sexual liberation movement. He believed in complete sexual freedom—that one should enjoy sex with multiple partners. At the time, he would have been a real advocate of the hookup culture. But years later, Leonard wrote a book ironically titled *The End of Sex: Erotic Love after the Sexual Revolution.* Leonard says, "I have finally come to see that every game has a rule, and sex has rules. Unless you play by the rules, you'll find sex can create a depth of loneliness that nothing else can." If Leonard's observation is correct, that sex has rules and ignoring these rules leads to painful consequences, then one must ask two simple questions: What are the rules and who makes them?

Personally, I think it starts with God because sex was His idea. And it seems only logical that if sex is God's idea, He must have a blueprint that leads to the ultimate sexual experience. Consider also: What if your ideas of sexuality are false? Where is that going to take you? Furthermore, what if you have a false understanding of what God really wants for you? What if it is not what you think?

So many people are convinced that God is the great spoiler of sexual pleasure. It is difficult for modern sophisticated people to believe that the biblical teaching on human sexuality offers the fullest, most satisfying sex life. God could have created sex strictly for the purpose of procreation without any pleasure whatsoever. But fortunately for us, he didn't. In fact, I would venture to say that if you will keep an open mind and read on, you will be shocked at what you discover and will agree that what God offers is the very best option for your sex life.

Our desires, including sexual desires, are not wrong. They are, rather, like the rungs of a ladder that lead us toward beauty, toward relationship and intimacy, and ultimately toward God who granted us these gifts. Remove the rungs from the ladder, though, and you are left with scattered sticks of wood leading nowhere.

Philip Yancey, Author

Chapter 7

THE PURPOSE
OF SEX

In her book *What are You Waiting For?*, Dannah Gresh shares some interesting insights on the issue of sex as found in the Old Testament. I was surprised to find such a predominant theme in the Bible.

In the Old Testament, when a man has sex with his wife, the English translation generally is, "he lays with her" or "has relations with her." But the actual Hebrew word for sex in the text is *yada*. In English, *yada* is a noun for "boring or empty talk." But in Hebrew, it is a verb: an action word that means "to know, to be known, to be deeply respected." Using the Hebrew definition, sexual intercourse is not just for pleasure, but rather its function or purpose is to know or be deeply known by someone. Gresh says that deep down, this is what every man and woman really yearns for.

She also points out a frequently used Hebrew word that is parallel to *yada*. It is the word *hesed*, which means "deep friendship, loyalty, devotion, and steadfastness." *Hesed* is faithful love; it also means kindness.

Not all sex is the same in the Old Testament. For example when David commits adultery with Bathsheba, the English text reads "he lay with her" (2 Sam. 11:4). However the Hebrew text does not use the word *yada* for sexual intercourse, but the Hebrew word *shakab*.

Gresh explains that *shakab* is a euphemism for sexual intercourse. She says it is often paired in the Hebrew language with the word *sikba,* which means "emission." In other words, *shakab* means "to exchange body fluids." This is what animals do and actually is a good description of hookup sex. And this, I believe, is precisely why so many students are finding the hookup culture to be so unfulfilling and meaningless.

In comparing world religions, Dr. Tim Keller describes the Bible as having the most glorious view of sex. He points out that, in Proverbs 5, husbands and wives are to be ravished with each other sexually. Then in the Song of Solomon, we witness a joyous and graphic celebration of sexual love and intimacy. Keller goes on to say that sex has a design, a purpose, and a goal. God intended sexual union as both a sign and a means of achieving life unity between two people. It is a means of expressing and a means of achieving complete life unity between husband and wife.

The difference between the sexual love that God desires for us and modern hookup sex is that one involves true love while the other is merely lust. Lust says, "I want your body, but I don't want you." When you love someone, you put that person before yourself and your desires. When you lust, all you want is pleasure. The other person is simply the necessary object to enable you to get what you want.

C. S. Lewis shares some great insight into this when he says to have sex without being married is to want pleasure without a commitment. It's like trying to taste and eat food and then vomiting it back up. In other words, a person wants to taste food but doesn't want it to become a part of them. This kind of thinking leads to bulimia, characterized by frequent episodes of binge eating, followed by frantic efforts to avoid gaining weight. It affects women and men of all ages. Bulimia ravages the human body because it separates taste from the actual digestion of the food. Essentially, you want all the pleasure but not the consequences of eating. You don't want the life-sustaining food.

Lewis argues that it is unnatural to extract physical pleasure from deep union between two people. To want pleasure without a purpose leads to alarming

consequences that will ravage you emotionally, psychologically, and spiritually.

Deep Connection

It is quite clear that God designed sexuality as a gift
to humanity because of our deep need for connection.
We yearn to have our souls deeply connected with someone else.

Author Donald Miller believes the words *alone, lonely,* and *loneliness* are three of the most powerful words in
the English language. These words reflect our humanity. Miller writes, "They are like the words 'hunger' and
'thirst.' But they are not words about the body; they are
words about the soul." Our souls have a deep longing
for connection with someone else, to have soul oneness.
All of us desire to be deeply and permanently connected
to someone else and to alleviate our loneliness. Remember the Hebrew understanding of sex: *yada:* to know, to
be known, and to be deeply loved and respected. *Yada*
allows us to be truly vulnerable, to be naked in both
body and soul.

To Cleave

God designed humans not only to connect with but also
to cleave to one another. In Matthew 19:4–5, Jesus quotes

from the Old Testament: "He who created them from the beginning made them male and female, and said for this reason a man shall leave his father and mother and cleave to his wife and the two shall become one flesh." The word *cleave* is an interesting Hebrew word. It means "absolute unity." Total unity. It is a deeply profound solidarity.

Tim Keller says it involves not simply a physical union but an emotional union, an economic union, a social

---

The difference between the sexual love that God desires for us and modern hookup sex is that one involves true love while the other is merely lust.

---

union. To cleave to someone is to say, "I completely belong to you. Exclusively! Permanently! Everything I have is yours. I am yours."

This is what marriage is, and this is why God created sex: for cleaving. Sex enables us to truly cleave to another person. God made sex to be able to say to one another, "I belong completely and exclusively and permanently to you. All of me. Everything."

Do you see how the hookup culture cheapens sexuality when it's just another form of recreation and pleasure that has no boundaries?

God is quite clear about this—you should never give someone your body if you have not given them your whole self. Otherwise, you are just an object for someone's pleasure. This is why you marry—radically giving yourself unconditionally to someone else, your

---

God made sex to be able to say to one another, "I belong completely and exclusively and permanently to you. All of me. Everything."

---

entire being. When you follow this prescription, your sex life will soar. When we settle for something less than God's blueprint, sex becomes routine, boring, and utterly meaningless.

What so many young people fail to take into account is that when we violate the sacredness of our own bodies, there are far-reaching ramifications that we are not aware of. When you sexually unite yourself with someone else, it impacts you relationally. Something happens between you and that person. The experience becomes a part of you. But when there is sex with no commitment, no boundaries, and multiple sex partners, it has the potential to drastically affect your life.

Several years ago, I heard a wonderful presentation on human sexuality given by a good friend. He spoke of a conversation he had with his college roommate when they were freshmen. The roommate was getting packed up and ready to leave for college. He knew that his dad wanted to talk to him, and this is how the conversation unfolded:

His father was quite the man. For two years he had been the captain of his college football team that had won two Rose Bowls in a row. He said "My dad was not a Christian, and didn't have a Biblical view of life, but he was a man's man." The son could tell that his father had something on his mind but was fumbling around and did not quite know what to say. The son finally asked: "Dad, is there something you want to say to me?" The father turned and took a deep breath and said, "Yeah there is, Son. I've never told you this before, but I think you should know. When I was in college and was the big man on campus, I could just about have any woman I wanted. And I did. I made my way sexually through many women. And the vast majority of them, I hate to say, I can't even remember their names. I had no idea who they were. But now I deeply regret it—because it's as if I carry around a piece of each of them in my soul. And at the most inopportune time their faces come back to haunt me. And they do haunt me." He said, "I've never spoken of this to your mother. But I think she knows it. Though she doesn't want to hear about it, she suspects my past. However, I believe what it does is prevent me from having the level of intimacy with your mom that I'd really like to have. It's a barrier that's between us. And so, I want to tell you just before leaving for school, if you can wait until you are married, I think you should."

The son was stunned to hear these words from his dad. But if you really think about it, his father was affirming a biblical truth, even though he didn't even realize it. He was advising his son to avoid his mistake because when two people have sexual intercourse, the two become one. A spiritual transfusion takes place. You now share a piece of the other person's soul, and you have given them a piece of yourself.

It is a temptation for women to tie their self-worth to outward physical beauty. They think, "Why should I care about my character when no one else does?"

Dr. Tim Keller, Author/Pastor

Chapter 8

REPRESSING OUR DESIRES . . . IS THAT HEALTHY?

Many of you probably can't fathom the thought of not having sex until you are married, because it sounds so unrealistic and repressive. For most college students and young singles, self-fulfillment is the rule of life. Each of us has a right to chart our individual course toward personal satisfaction and happiness, and it is very natural for us to reason that sexual gratification is essential to personhood. For clarity purposes let's consider this question: "What should determine what is sexually right, moral, and good—God's truth or my desires?"

It's easy for college students to believe that the quality of their social life is everything. For many, that's actually the reason for going to college. It's common to fall into the belief that drinking, partying, and then hooking up are essential to finding a happy college experience. However, research is leading many college mental health professionals to a different conclusion. They are now seeing that the modern college lifestyle is creating a multitude of problems in the lives of students, to the point that many young men and women are finding themselves ill-prepared to enter adulthood. But if you look back in history, you will see that today's young adult is not necessarily an aberration.

A History of Happiness

Several years ago, Dr. Darrin McMahon, a professor at Florida State University, wrote a landmark book on a history of the pursuit of happiness. He basically describes the different approaches people have taken over the years in their search for a happy life. Most people naturally believe that a life filled with pleasure will lead to happiness. Pleasure generally makes us feel good, and good feelings are a major component of living a happy life. For this reason, we equate happiness with pleasure.

It was Sigmund Freud who came along and said that when you look at people's lives, their only purpose is to be happy and that genital sex is the primary source of all human happiness. Many believe it is Freud's teachings that gave rise to the sexual revolution of the 1960s and have vastly influenced today's view of sex. But what most people do not realize is that Freud's views on sex and sexual boundaries took an apparent shift. He said when sexual

---

> When we think of character, we generally think of honesty, integrity, diligence, fairness, and selflessness. But at the heart of character is the ability to restrain one's desires.

---

standards disappear, the same thing happens to us that happened "in the decline of ancient civilization, [when] love became worthless and life empty." Surprisingly, Freud actually raised his children with clear-cut sexual boundaries. Dr. Armand Nicholi has studied and written on the life of Freud. He says we can only speculate, but it seems Freud concluded later in life that finding happiness in this world requires a great deal of self-restraint.

Over the centuries, most social critics have concluded that the pursuit of happiness through pleasure can bring a lot of delight into your life, but not lasting happiness. As in the life of Oscar Wilde, which we looked at in chapter 2, the demand for pleasure is forever at war with reality. It has the potential to enslave you and then destroy you.

In McMahon's book there is a second approach to the pursuit of happiness that is not as obvious to modern people and is somewhat counterintuitive. It is the

> In sacrifice, [something is not being taken away from you. You are not being deprived. Rather,] you are making a choice to give up something of lesser value right now in order to experience something more wonderful and meaningful and of greater value in the future.

path of virtue. It is to develop a life of strong character. McMahon says this is more of an age-old approach, "tying happiness to higher things: to God, virtue, or the right ordering of the soul." Happiness is considered a reward for living well.

Most people know that Thomas Jefferson is the author of the Declaration of Independence and that in the written documents are the famous words that guarantee the rights of all citizens to "Life, Liberty and the pursuit of Happiness." In reference to the word *happiness,* Jefferson had this to say: "Happiness is the aim of life, but virtue is the foundation of happiness." Benjamin Franklin, one of the signers of the declaration, said, "Virtue and happiness are mother and daughter." In other words, they believed you can never find happiness without virtue.

C. S. Lewis, who was a scholar in both classical and medieval literature, also saw the importance of virtue in the search for happiness and the good life. In fact, Lewis in the *Chronicles of Narnia* and J.R.R. Tolkien in *The Lord of the Rings* emphasize the need for people to have character and virtue in order to live in a complex and confusing world. Happiness will never be found unless people know how to rise to the moral challenges around them.

Unfortunately, little emphasis is placed on a life of virtue and character today. In fact, most college students will give you a blank stare should you try to engage them in a conversation about this issue. Christian Smith, a professor of sociology at Notre Dame, recently asked a group of students to name the most recent moral dilemma they were faced with. Seventy percent could not even come up with one. Smith pressed these students for an answer, and most of them replied, "What feels right for me is moral for me, and if it feels right for you, then it is moral for you." This is the way most college students view morality.

Journalist David Brooks says we have lost our vocabulary on how to talk about character. This is particularly true of young people. Brooks once queried several professors at Princeton, "Do you instill character in your students?" Though they understood the need for students to develop character, they acknowledged they had no idea how to teach it to them. Additionally, although I am sure parents want their children to grow up and be people of strong character, they are very much like Ivy League professors—they don't know how to teach them either.

So what does it mean to be a man or woman of character? Historically, people of strong character recognize that there is a universal moral standard to live by and that it enables them to determine what is right and wrong. A person of character is naturally inclined to do the right thing, even if everyone else is going in a different direction. Virtuous people are generally the most courageous because, more often than not, they are traveling down lonely roads in order to do what's right. When we think of character, we generally think of honesty, integrity, diligence, fairness, and selflessness. But at the heart of character is the ability to restrain one's desires. As a person grows in character, he or she is building muscles of restraint.

Furthermore, our character serves as a compass that guides us through life. It ultimately defines who we are and how we live our lives. Those who have little character find themselves lost in this life with no compass and

> "What women will and will not permit does have a profound way of influencing the behavior of an entire society."

with no sense of direction. This is what seems to happen with college students who are completely immersed in the hookup culture.

Ravi Zacharias describes such a man who made some very bad choices in his sexual life. This man had convinced himself that what he had indulged in was really a need in his life. He said, "The more I convinced myself that I needed it, I soon redefined who I was as a person. Now, as I look at what I have become, I can no longer live with myself. I hate who I am. I am emotionally running, but I do not know where to go."

This is what seems to happen with college students who are completely emerged in the hookup culture. They have no idea who they are and where their lives are headed. The words of Dr. Laura Schlesinger, a noted therapist best describe the cost of abandoning one's character:

> The great mistake of modern man is to confuse pleasurable experience (and feeling good) with happiness. After 20 years of counseling, I can tell you that the main thrust of too many lives is an over-emphasis on feeling good than living wisely. In the process, a life of character is often abandoned for the pursuit of self-gratification. The result is a life full of thrills and good feelings, but eventually it is accompanied by a host of destructive consequences. Yet people will continue to make that trade-off and then will complain bitterly about the price they have to pay.

Making Sense of It All

To truly understand the great transformation that has taken place in our views and beliefs about sexuality, one must go back almost 2,700 years to a single sentence uttered by the Old Testament prophet Isaiah. His words seem timeless, as if they were written for us today. He says:

"Woe to those who call evil good, and good, evil; who substitute darkness for light, and light for darkness; who substitute bitter for sweet, and sweet for bitter!" (Isaiah 5:20). This is what has happened to us. This is precisely what the media, Hollywood, and those who create our entertainment have done. They have taken what God has said is healthy, what is beautiful, and what is good, and they have made it appear to be antiquated, boring, and uninteresting. God's laws are in place for a reason, but the secular world minimizes the consequences of sex and overstates its benefits. The secular world has taken what God has said is wrong, evil, and unhealthy and has made it appear to be exciting and intriguing.

When was the last time you saw a movie or television show where a married couple has a healthy, loving relationship and sex life? Hollywood loves to highlight dysfunctional relationships, infidelity, and sex that has no boundaries, and people believe that this somehow makes for an exciting, magical life. Just one example is the way in which most college students react when they hear the phrase *sexual purity*. Most respond with some wisecrack, particularly if someone is suggesting it for them. They think it is so prudish and outdated. But what the word *purity* means might actually be surprising. Elizabeth Elliott shares some profound words about purity, particularly in the context of human sexuality. She writes:

> Purity means freedom from contamination, from anything that would spoil the taste or pleasure, reduce the power, or in any way cheapen what the thing was meant to be. It means cleanness; clearness; no additives; nothing artificial; in other words, all natural; in the sense in which the Designer designed it to be.

As I read this, several words caught my attention— *contamination* and the phrase *reduce the power*. When you think of the future, when you think of your future with your spouse, your soul mate, do you want to risk contaminating and reducing the power of your future sex life? Because this is what's at stake. And as I read that for the first time, I thought, "This is really what I want for my children." Then it struck me that this is also what I want for my marriage. This is what God offers when we live our lives in harmony with His design.

Deprivation versus Sacrifice

You may be thinking, "You don't really expect me to deprive myself and wait until I am married until I have sex? It's just not reasonable for me to wait until my spouse comes along. I can't deprive myself of this wonderful pleasure. It is just not possible!"

When you deprive yourself of something, it means a possession or pleasure is taken away from you. But let's consider this belief from an entirely different point of view. Waiting to give yourself to someone when you get married should be seen as a sacrifice—a joyful sacrifice. You see, *sacrifice* means giving up something you highly value for the sake of something of even greater value. Sacrifice is such a beautiful concept because it involves purpose. It acknowledges a goal that is worthier and of greater value than what is being sacrificed. In sacrifice, something is not being taken away from you. You are not being deprived. Rather, you are making a choice to give up something of lesser value right now in order to experience something more wonderful and meaningful and of greater value in the future.

James Q. Wilson confirms this idea in his book *The Moral Sense*. He tells us "that the best things in life will cost you something. We must sacrifice to attain them, to achieve them, to keep them, and to enjoy them."

Popular lecturer Cliff Knechtle says:

> Self-control is not repressive or psychologically hazardous when a person is aiming for a valuable prize. When the goal is sufficiently worthy, self-control is not an evil—it's a part of the realistic process of achieving that goal. When we realize that the all-wise God is good, and He loves us, then we understand that it is beneficial to exercise self-control in the use of our sexuality.

What Is Sexy?

To conclude this chapter let's look at some words from an op-ed piece written in *Newsweek* magazine several years ago, titled "Modesty Is Sexy. Really." The author is Pulitzer Prize–winning journalist George Will. He critiques a book by Wendy Shalit, *A Return to Modesty: Discovering the Lost Virtue.* Shalit questions whether women are better off now than they were before the sexual revolution. She contends women are naturally modest; it is a part of their wiring, so to speak. Sexual modesty is a reflex that arises from their femininity, and women should stubbornly resist the sexual presumptuousness that men display toward them. Shalit says that young men have no clue how to relate to real women. A strong woman should say to the world, "I am worth waiting for. So I am not going to give myself to you, not to you, not you, and not you, either." But this type of thinking is so foreign to young women who have been swept up by the hookup culture.

Shalit believes it's time for women to return to sexual modesty. Women should be proud to be sexually hesitant, and their hesitancy should arise from the mature hope for a dignified relationship with one man. She makes an observation that is worthy of bold print: "**what women will and will not permit does have a profound way of influencing the behavior of an entire society.**"

This profound statement is a real compliment to the power and command women can have in this culture. They, particularly, have the ability to influence the behavior of immature college men. Shalit believes if they would form a "cartel of virtue," it would lead to educating young men about what it means to have a meaningful relationship with a woman. They might also learn that a woman's body and sexual intimacy is something that is considered to be very sacred. Women would no longer be an object for men's pleasure, but persons of great value and worth.

Shalit concludes her article by making a compelling argument that women who are modest and moral are the sexiest. Ironically, men find them to be incredibly attractive. Admittedly, most guys in college and in their single years will have sex with any woman who is willing to consent. But when it comes to choosing a wife, they don't want a woman who has slept around. In fact, Wendy Shalit would tell all women, "Don't be fools. Don't spend your college years being used as a pawn in the hands of young men and in the process ending up with a lifetime of regret."

Finally, Shalit, who apparently does not speak from a Christian perspective, appeals to our logic when it comes to sexual restraint. She says saving yourself sexually "may even be the proof of God because it means that we have been designed in such a way that when we humans act like animals, without any restraint and without any rules, we just don't have as much fun."

Meaning is one of the greatest needs of human life, one of our deepest hungers, and perhaps in the final analysis, the most basic need in the realm of human experience."

Dr. Dallas Willard, College Philosophy Professor

Chapter 9

WHY ARE
WE HERE?

When the book *Unprotected* was first published, the name of the author was not on the cover. Instead, the cover showed the book was written by Dr. Anonymous. The author was Dr. Miriam Grossman, who knew her message was not popular, particularly among her colleagues. She feared professional and employment reprisals because of her candid views about what she saw happening in the lives of sexually promiscuous young women. College psychiatrists are expected to embrace the modern ideology that casual sex has no negative circumstances, but she recognized how dishonest this view was, based on what she was observing in the very lives of her patients.

Grossman (who eventually let it be known that she was the author of this excellent book) observes that many of her student patients really seek to do the right things. They eat well, exercise, and structure their lives around their studies. But no one ever taught them to be healthy when it comes to their sexuality. Here's one of her many examples. Heather struggled with depression but never thought that it was because she had a "friend-with-benefits" relationship with a young man at UCLA. It finally dawned on her that they were not good friends, yet he was still receiving the benefits of a sexual relationship with her. Apparently, Heather had not been told that for women, there is an increased risk for depression when they participate in casual sexual relationships.

Grossman then began to realize that college health and counseling centers focus on promoting health through diet, exercise, sleep, physical exams, not smoking, and using condoms, but they never encourage students to consider ways to nurture their souls.

She believes students are finally realizing that they have a soul, and this fact has been completely neglected by mental health professionals. Grossman also believes that over three-fourths of college students are on a spiritual search. This may sound like a large percentage of the student population, but she says it is consistent with the research that indicates we are meaning-seeking creatures. And clearly, we are. Several years ago, *USA Today* published the results of a survey they had conducted by asking a large group of people, "If you could ask God one question and He would give you an answer, what would you ask Him?" The number one response in the survey was "I would like to ask God why I am here. What is the reason for my existence?"

This should not surprise us, because people throughout the ages have asked this question, going all the way back to the early Greek philosophers. The Greeks believed in a concept called the *logos*. It literally means *word*, but it has an important secondary meaning: *reason* or *reason for life*. The Greek philosophers were in search for the *logos*, the reason for life. They believed when you found it, you would be whole, complete, and fulfilled. The problem is, they could never agree on the "logos." They could never come up with a unified answer.

The dilemma is a real problem for people living in this modern world, particularly college students. Several years ago, Billy Graham was visiting Derek Bok, who at the time was the President of Harvard University. After their meeting, and as Graham was leaving, he asked Bok one final question: "What do you think is the number one problem the students at Harvard struggle with?" Bok did not have to think long about his answer. "Living with emptiness. Living purposeless, meaningless lives." Kelly Kulberg, founder of the Veritas Forum at Harvard, responded to President Bok's answer to Graham:

"Unwittingly, he had offered an explanation for the rise of depression, sexual confusion, transmitted disease, drug use, binge drinking, pornography, and even suicide." She then asks a very penetrating question: "How did our great universities become places of emptiness?"

Can Purpose Be Found?

In chapter 3, I mention a famous Pulitzer Prize–winning book written by Ernest Becker. In *The Denial of Death,* Becker argues that God is irrelevant in people's lives today. As a result, we now believe we are here by accident, we do not have any real purpose in life, and we are seeking something to give us a sense of significance. He goes on to say that modern people are looking to sex and romance to get a sense of meaning that we used to get from God. Many people believe God exists but that He has no relevance in their day-to-day living. We have pushed God out of our lives. But can we really expect to find true purpose and meaning in our lives without Him? Think about the word *purpose.* What does it mean to you? One of the best ways to grasp it is with a visual. Pull out your smart phone. Would you not agree that it is more than a blob of worthless plastic? It has a purpose. It did not pop into existence by itself or by accident. It clearly has a skillful designer who brought it into being. The point is that purpose implies design. But naturally, in order to have a design, you must have a designer.

When you look at a smart phone, its purpose for existence is plainly evident. But when you look at a human being, it is not as clear. For this reason, we must look to God, our Designer, to answer the questions: What was I designed to do, and what is the purpose of my life?

I have found that the answers to these questions are crucial because when we operate as we were designed, we function well in our individual lives and in our relationships. When we fail to function as we were designed, we malfunction.

Design for Living

Think about the desires of the body. When we are born, we have three basic physical needs: hunger, thirst, and sleep. We get hungry and so we eat; we get thirsty so we drink; and when we get tired, we rest. And somewhere during adolescence, puberty hits, and our sexual desire is ignited. What has happened throughout the ages, but particularly in modern times, is that we have elevated these four desires of the body, these sensual desires, to the point that they have begun to dominate our lives. For many people, satisfying these desires provides the basic reason for living.

But we are more than just a body. We have a soul that has certain needs and desires, and it is our souls that long for the intangibles of life. It is our souls that long for purpose and meaning, as well as for love, joy, and peace. Do you see what is happening in our culture today? People are attempting to satisfy the spiritual longings of the soul with the physical pleasures of life, specifically sex, and it is not working. The spiritual longings of the soul can be satisfied only by God Himself.

So for the sake of argument, let's consider what the Bible says about our design. First, we are told that we are designed in the image of God. Therfore, we possess a number of God's own characteristics. He designed us with emotions and personalities. He gave us the ability to think, reason, and be creative—characteristics that none of His other creatures possess. Moreover, we are relational beings and have the ability to love. We are the only creatures God designed that He could love, and we could return that love in a meaningful way. The Bible also tells us that He made us for Himself. We exist for Him, not for ourselves. God created us to live in a love relationship with Him. This is why the words of Augustine ring so true: "You have made us for Yourself and our hearts will not find rest until we rest in Thee."

I once saw a youth director demonstrate this in a very effective way. In front of a group of teenagers, he put a goldfish bowl on a small table. The bowl was full of water with a single goldfish in it. He proceeded to stick his hand down into the bowl, picked up the goldfish, and then dropped it on the table. The fish jumped two feet into the air, then off the table and onto the floor.

Then it jumped all over the floor until it finally lay still, as its gills strained for oxygen. As you can imagine, the girls begged him to put the fish back in the bowl, which he finally did. Then he explained to them that a fish can soar in life and truly be a fish only in water. In addition, just as a fish is made for water, we were made for God. We are designed to live in a relationship with Him.

The Great Deception

According to C. S. Lewis, human beings over the centuries have looked for all types of ways to invent happiness for themselves outside of God, and it is out of these hopeless attempts that we have produced so much misery in the world. Lewis describes "the long, terrible story of man trying to find something other than God which will make him happy." Then he gives a logical explanation why it will never work:

> The reason why it can never succeed is this. God made us: invented us as a man invents an engine. A car is made to run on gasoline, and it would not properly on anything else. God designed humans to run on Himself. He Himself is the fuel our spirits were designed to burn, the food our spirits were designed to feed on. There is no other. That is why it is no good just asking God to make us happy in our own way, without bothering about [having a relationship

with Him]. God cannot give us a happiness and peace apart from Himself, because it is not there. There is no such thing.

The Woman at the Well

One of the most interesting personal encounters that Jesus has with an individual is found in the fourth chapter of the book of John. He is by Himself at a well, and a woman comes to draw water. They have a conversation, and then Christ begins to focus on her spiritual needs. He offers her "living water" so that she will never thirst again. He is actually telling her that He could satisfy the deepest longing in her soul. She responds by telling Jesus that she wants this living water.

Out of the blue, He asks her a very unusual question: "Where is your husband?" She proceeds to tell him she has no husband. He responds by telling her, "You have spoken the truth; you have had five husbands, and the man you are now living with is not your husband." Why would Jesus, in the midst of explaining to this woman of the spiritual need in her life, ask about her dysfunctional relationships with men? It seems obvious that this woman had been looking to satisfy the deep longing of her soul with sex and romance, yet it had utterly failed her. Christ is telling her, and us, that we will live our lives with unfulfilled longing and a deep unquenchable thirst unless He Himself is the anchor of our souls.

Every single one of us needs to build our lives on something solid and secure, and until we find this foundation, we cannot really begin to live properly. We cannot satisfy the deep longing of the soul. C. S. Lewis demonstrates this truth powerfully in one of his stories in the *Chronicles of Narnia*. The Narnia books are a series of allegorical children's stories, yet they speak powerfully to the lives of adults as well. A young girl named Jill in Lewis's book *The Silver Chair* presents a wonderful representation of humanity. She is clearly consumed with herself and is convinced that she alone knows what is best for her life. She wants to have nothing to do with Aslan, the powerful and magnificent lion who represents Christ. Yet Jill is desperately searching for water:

> Jill grows unbearably thirsty. She can hear a stream somewhere in the forest. Driven by her thirst, she begins to look for this source of water—cautiously, because she is fearful of running into the Lion. She finds the stream, but she is paralyzed by what she sees there: Aslan, huge and golden, still as a statue but terribly alive, is sitting beside the water. She waits for a long time, wrestling with her thoughts and hoping that he'll just go away.
>
> Then Aslan says, "If you are thirsty, you may drink."
>
> Jill is startled and refuses to come closer.
>
> "Are you not thirsty?" said the Lion.

"I am dying of thirst," said Jill.

"Then drink," said the Lion.

"May I—could I—would you mind going away while I do?" said Jill.

The Lion answered this only by a look and a very low growl. And just as Jill gazed at its motionless hulk, she realized that she might as well have asked the whole mountain to move aside for her convenience.

The delicious rippling noise of the stream was driving her near frantic.

"Will you promise not to—do anything to me, if I come?"

"I will make no promise," said the Lion.

Jill was so thirsty now that, without noticing it, she had come a step nearer.

"Do you eat girls?" she said.

"I have swallowed up girls and boys, women and men, kings and emperors, cities and realms," said the Lion. It didn't say this as if it were boasting, nor as if it were sorry, nor as if it were angry. It just said it.

"I daren't come and drink," said Jill.

"Then you will die of thirst," said the Lion.

"Oh dear!" said Jill, coming another step nearer. "I suppose I must go and look for another stream then."

"There is no other stream," said the Lion.

What I have found is that so many people spend their entire lives looking for some other stream to finally and forever quench the thirst of their souls. I would encourage you to look at your own life. What have you been looking to, to quench the longing of your soul? Be honest—how is it working for you? Jesus is very clear: there is no other stream. There is no other fountain of living water.

What I find to be most interesting is that if you read the entire Bible, what you will find at the very end, in the last chapter in the book of Revelation, in one of the very last verses, is an invitation. It is an invitation that God offers to each of us: "Whoever is thirsty, let him come; and whoever wishes, let him take of the free gift of the water of life" (Revelation 22:17). Will we take it? Will we drink, or will we continue to look fruitlessly for some other stream?

"After twenty years of listening to the yearnings of people's hearts, I am convinced that human beings have an inborn desire for God. Whether we are consciously religious or not, this desire is our deepest longing and most precious treasure."

Dr. Gerald May, psychiatrist

Epilogue

The data seems clear that a person's spiritual life can have a significant impact on his or her mental well-being and that there is a powerful relationship between a young person's sexual conduct and the level of happiness he or she experiences

Dr. Armand Nicholi, mentioned previously, is a clinical professor of psychiatry at Harvard Medical School. For thirty-five years, he taught a course for Harvard undergraduates, comparing the life and worldview of Sigmund Freud with those of C. S. Lewis.

Nicholi is the editor and co-author of the classic *The Harvard Guide to Psychiatry*, which we looked at in chapter 5. As you will recall, there is a chapter in it titled "The Adolescent." In that section, he detailed some of the destructive psychological and health consequences of youth sexual promiscuity. From the clinical research, it is quite clear that sexual permissiveness has led to empty relationships and feelings of worthlessness. Many of these students were desperately attempting to overcome a profound sense of loneliness. Nicholi says these students "described pervasive feelings of guilt and haunting concerns that they were using others and being used as sexual objects."

In his bestselling book, *The Question of God,* Nicholi shares how many of the students at Harvard became disillusioned with their sex lives. As a result, he began to notice a trend toward spiritual revival among some of the students who had been involved in his research on adolescence, many of whom had become Christians. They concluded that their sexual relationships were not at all satisfactory and did not provide the closeness they desired. But once they had become Christians, they attempted to live by the biblical standard. Though these new standards conflicted with their past behavior, Nicholi says, "they found these clear-cut boundaries less confusing than no boundaries at all and helpful in relating to members of the opposite sex "as persons rather than sexual objects." It led to a real transformation in their lives.

We Are All Guilty

Most people don't realize it, but most of us have been guilty of sexual sin. Whether in the flesh or the imagination, we are all likely sexually fallen creatures. Therefore, we all have a universal need to receive God's mercy and forgiveness, but we also need His transforming power operating in our lives.

When you read the four gospels that document the life of Christ, you see Him interact with all types of people. There are times, particularly with the religious Pharisees, that you see Him speak with anger and harsh words. However, very often you see Him speak very tender words of great compassion. On two different occasions, Jesus encounters two women who are clearly guilty of sexual sin. In both instances you see His compassion toward them.

The first is the woman at the well in John 4 whose story we discussed in the last chapter. She had been married five times and was currently living with a man. You see no criticism or condemnation about her marriages or even her current living situation. He offers her living water for her thirsty soul, which is what she really longed for and desperately needed. Then, in John, chapter 8, Jesus meets the adulterous woman, whom the scribes and Pharisees actually brought to Him, throwing her at His feet. They demanded she be stoned to death, but what they really wanted to see was whether He agreed with their verdict. John describes what happens next:

> When they persisted in asking Him, He straightened up and He said to them, "he who is without sin among you, let him be the first to throw a stone at her." And again He stooped down and wrote on the ground, and when they heard it they began to go out one by one, beginning with the older ones. And He was left alone; and the woman, where she was in the midst. And straightening up Jesus said to her, "Woman, where are they? Did no one condemn you?" And she said, "no one, Lord" and Jesus said, "neither do I condemn you. Go your way. From now on, sin no more." (John 4:7–11)

Here you see no condemnation. Jesus does not even chastise her for her adulterous acts. But also notice that He doesn't say, "Go and follow the desires and passions of your body." He said, "Go and sin no more." Remember, He designed our sexuality, but He clearly knows that when we just follow the lusts of our bodies, it keeps us from realizing the very best He has for us.

Finally a word of compassion for those of you who might be experiencing guilt and shame from your past. Christ not wants only to forgive you but to heal you and restore you. As we learn in Psalm 23, He wants to restore our souls. I love the word *restore*. It means to take that which is damaged and broken and to make it as if it is brand new—to restore it to its original design. This is what Christ desires to do in each of our lives.

But He also desires for us to follow Him—to allow Him to lead us through life. Let Him lead you to your intended spouse. In the end, I can promise you that if you will allow Him to do this, He will give you the very best.

Sources

Becker, Ernest. *The Denial of Death*. New York: Free Press Paperbacks, Simon & Schuster, 1973.

Budziszewski, J. *How to Stay Christian in College*. Colorado Springs: Think Books, NavPress, 2004.

Buford, Bob. "Of Two Minds about Civilization," My Next Book Year 9, Chapter 8, August 6, 2013, http://leadnet.org/my_next_book_year_9_chapter_8_of_two_minds_about_civilization/.

Covey, Stephen R. *The Seven Habits of Highly Effective People: Restoring the Character Ethic*. New York: Fireside, Simon & Schuster Inc., 1989.

Elliot, Elisabeth. *Passion and Purity*. Old Tappan, NJ: Fleming H. Revell Company, 1984.

Freitas, Donna. *The End of Sex: How Hookup Culture Is Leaving a Generation Unhappy, Sexually Unfulfilled, and Confused about Intimacy*. New York: Basic Books, Perseus Books Group, 2013.

Glynn, Patrick. *God, The Evidence: The Reconciliation of Faith and Reason in a Postsecular World*. New York: Three Rivers Press, 1997.

Gresh, Dannah. *What Are You Waiting For? The One Thing No One Ever Tells You about Sex.* Colorado Springs: WaterBrook Press, 2011.

Grossman, M.D., Miriam. *Unprotected: A Campus Psychiatrist Reveals How Political Correctness in Her Profession Endangers Every Student.* New York: Penguin Group, 2006.

Hall, Laurie. *An Affair of the Mind.* Carol Stream., IL: Wheaton: Tyndale House Publishers, 1996.

Keller, Tim. Selected Sermons: "Lust; The Case of Joseph," 3/12/95; "Sex and the End of Loneliness," 11/5/06; "Love and Lust," 5/6/12; and "Sex and the Romantic Solution," 5/8/14.

Knechtle, Cliffe. *Help Me Believe: Direct Answers to Real Questions.* Downers Grove, IL: InterVarsity Press, 2000.

Kullberg, Kelly Monroe. *Finding God beyond Harvard: The Quest for Veritas.* Downers Grove, IL: IVP Books, InterVarsity Press, 2006.

Lewis, C. S. *The Chronicles of Narnia (The Silver Chair Book 4):* New York: Harper Trophy, HarperCollins Publishers, 1953.

Lewis, C.S. *Mere Christianity: An Anniversary Edition of the Three Books: The Case for Christianity, Christian Behavior, and Beyond Personality.* New York: Macmillan Publishing Co., Inc., 1981.

Maltz, Wendy and Larry Maltz. *The Porn Trap: The Essential Guide to Overcoming Problems Caused by Pornography*. New York: Harper, 2008.

McGrath, Alister. *If I Had Lunch with C. S. Lewis: Exploring the Ideas of C. S. Lewis on the Meaning of Life*. Carol Stream, IL: Tyndale House Publishers, 2014.

McMahon, Darrin M. *Happiness: A History*. New York: Grove Press, 2006.

Miller, Donald. *Blue Like Jazz: Nonreligious Thoughts on Christian Spirituality*. Nashville: Thomas Nelson Publishers, 2003.

Morris, Thomas. *Making Sense of It All: Pascal and the Meaning of Life*. Grand Rapids: Wm. B. Eerdmans Publishing, 1992.

Nabers Jr., Drayton. *The Case for Character: Looking at Character from a Biblical Perspective*. Tulsa: Christian Publishing Services, 2006.

Nicholi Jr., Dr. Armand M. *The Question of God: C.S. Lewis and Sigmund Freud Debate God, Love, Sex, and the Meaning of Life*. New York: Free Press, 2002.

Paul, Pamela. *Pornified: How Pornography Is Damaging Our Lives, Our Relationships, and Our Families*. New York: Holt Paperbacks, Henry Holt and Company, 2005.

Stockman, Steve. *Walk On: The Spiritual Journey of U2*. Orlando: Relevant Books, Relevant Media Group, Inc. 2005.

Will, George F. "Modesty Is Sexy. Really." *Newsweek* (February 1, 1999), 74.

Winner, Lauren F. *Realsex: The Naked Truth about Chastity.* Grand Rapids: Brazos Press, 2005.

Wolf, Naomi. "The Porn Myth." *New York* magazine (October 20, 2003).

Yancey, Philip. *Finding God in Unexpected Places.* New York: Doubleday, Random House, 2005.

———. "Not Naked Enough." *Christianity Today* (February 19, 1990), 48.

———. *Rumors of Another World: What on Earth Are We Missing?* Grand Rapids: Zondervan, 2003.

———. *What Good Is God?: In Search of a Faith That Matters.* New York: FaithWords, 2010.

Zacharias, Ravi. *Recapture the Wonder.* Nashville: Integrity Publishers, 2003.

About the Author

Richard E. Simmons III is the founder and executive director for The Center for Executive Leadership, a not-for-profit, faith-based ministry located in Birmingham, AL. Simmons opened the center in 2000 to assist men in the development of their faith through formal bible studies, teaching and counseling while also overseeing a talented group of professional and personal counselors.

Simmons received his B.A. from the University of the South (Sewanee) in Economics in 1976. He later studied Risk Management and Insurance at Georgia State prior to beginning a 25-year career with Hilb, Rogal, and Hamilton, a property and casualty insurance firm where he was CEO for ten years. Much of Simmons' life has been devoted to giving back to the community by advising businessmen and professionals. Through these experiences, he discovered he had a calling for teaching, writing and public speaking.

Richard and his beautiful wife Holly, have 3 children and they reside in Birmingham, AL.

Safe Passage

Thinking Clearly About Life And Death

"This book examines C.S. Lewis's thoughts and perspective on the issue of human mortality."

- Richard E. Simmons III

WWW.THECENTERBHAM.ORG

The True Measure of a Man

How Perceptions of Success, Achievement & Recognition Fail Men in Difficult Times

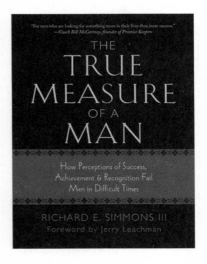

"In our performance driven culture, this book provides liberating truth on how to be set free from the fear of failure, comparing ourselves to others, and the false ideas we have about masculinity."

- Richard E. Simmons III

WWW.THECENTERBHAM.ORG

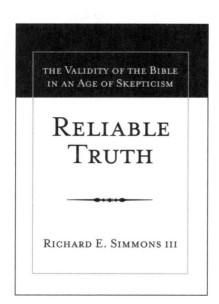

Reliable Truth

The Validity of the Bible in an Age of Skepticism

"This book offers powerful and compelling evidence why the Bible is valid and true."

- Richard E. Simmons III

WWW.THECENTERBHAM.ORG

A Life of Excellence

Wisdom for Effective Living

"This book lays out three principles that clearly point to a life of excellence. I am convinced that if one lives in accordance with these principles, his or her life will flourish and prosper."

- Richard E. Simmons III

WWW.THECENTERBHAM.ORG